Secret Genealogy V
Black, White and Hamite; Ancestors of Color in Our Family Trees
by
Suellen Ocean

Secret Genealogy V
Black, White and Hamite; Ancestors of Color in Our Family Trees

by
Suellen Ocean

Published by:
Ocean-Hose
P.O. Box 115
Grass Valley, CA 95945
www.oceanhose.com

Also by Suellen Ocean:
Secret Genealogy
Secret Genealogy II
Secret Genealogy III
Secret Genealogy IV
The Lies of the Lion
The Guild
The Celtic Prince
Black Pansy
Blue Violet
Black Lilac
Gold River
Gone North
Chimney Fire
Hot Snow
Acorns And Eat'em
Poor Jonny's Cookbook

Table of Contents

Quote

"I do not plead here this evening for emigration to Africa. The time has not come, if indeed it ever will come, for the American Negro to emigrate to Africa. This is our home, this is our land, this is our country. The strong arm of our fathers cleared its forests, disemboweled its hills, and tunneled its mountains. Their toil, their sweat, their tears, their blood have enriched its soil. Here our dead are buried. Here we are bound by the most sacred ties that ever touched or stirred or thrilled a human soul. We are American citizens..."

M. C. B. Mason, D.D. Assistant Corresponding Secretary Freedmen's Aid and Southern Education Society, 1895

Chapter One

Colonial Admixture

I wonder about the women who came before me in my family tree. What color was their hair? Were they slender and delicate or were they strong and stout, able to work right alongside the men in the corn fields and apple orchards? Were they soft-hearted and kind or were they mean and bitter?

We did not arrive in this world alone. We are a link in a chain that goes back millions of years. And being the curious people that we are, we want to know... what did the people in that chain look like? What has become of them? Do they inhabit the *otherworld?* And from that world, do they somehow communicate with us so we can uncover their stories? Or is it enough that they've left us clues to trace their steps in *this world?*

Thirty years ago, I took a sociology class where the professor kept saying: *there is no such thing as race*. Ever since, I've had a hard time using that word. Forensic anthropologists might not agree with the concept of race either, but they are repeatedly asked to determine the "race" of a deceased individual. It's their job and they are very good at it. But in their field, there are serious discussions over the concept of race, and a growing awareness that it *has no biological basis*. The belief is that people are different colors because of environmental and genetic influences *not* because they belong to different "races."

When we "do" genealogy, we usually study written records. Photographs can be non-existent so we can't go by looks alone. This presents a problem, because what I'm looking for, is any sign that my recent ancestors (since the colonial era) were African. Furthermore, anthropologists say that we look different today morphologically (the form and structure of our features) than our ancestors did during the colonial era.

When studying these groups; American Indian, Caucasian, Polynesian, Negroid and Mongoloid, forensic anthropologists found that the *midface region* is the best part of the face to determine a skeleton's "race." It's interesting to note though, because of "admixture," forensic scientists are predicting that tomorrow's anthropologists will have a harder time telling the difference between a black and a white skeleton.

The skeletons of European **Americans** from the 1800s are similar in form and structure to that of simply European skeletons from the same time period. But by the 1900's there was much more disparity between them. In the African group, today's African **Americans** differ greatly from African **Americans** from the 1800's. Add to that, anthropological studies that reveal that **today's** European **Americans** and African **Americans** are more like each other morphologically than they are to their ancestors of the colonial era. Over the years we have become closely related, due to admixture (the mixing of the gene pool).

Throughout history, having babies out of wedlock was a big secret. Having a bi-racial baby was an even bigger secret. For centuries, bi-racial marriages in America were forbidden. The Slave Code of Louisiana (1724-1803) prohibited "white subjects, of both sexes, to marry with the

3

blacks…" and forbade "all our white subjects, and even the manumitted or free-born blacks, to live in a state of concubinage with blacks." If there was an "issue" that arose from one of these "forbidden" relationships, (the issue being a child born) that child was to be "adjudged to the hospital of the locality, and said slaves shall be forever incapable of being set free." So they took the baby away and placed it in the closest hospital with the parents suffering the consequence of never being set free.

If you're working on your family history and you suspect there's a secret, good luck trying to get the older relatives to speak up. Too often, that secret was buried and will stay buried. No one has ever given me reason to believe that my family history has one of these secrets but I suspect it does. There are a lot of people in a three-hundred-year-old family tree and undoubtedly a lot of secrets. I am pleased that Louisiana is digitizing their old hospital records because as the Slave Code of Louisiana tells us, the hospital is where the baby was sent. But no doubt, as soon as the baby was old enough, it was released into the world as a slave.

If I could change history, I would. There is much about it that offends me. Seeking ancestors who were slaves requires digging through an era that is so horrifying, I presume most people don't delve too deep. Researching colonial slavery can leave one feeling downcast. But I hope this research helps you in your search to find the true origins of your ancestors and brings insight to your world of genealogy.

Even though other countries besides America had their hand in slavery, there was strong opposition to it. In the years leading up to the Civil War, British citizens sent donations to abolitionists to help free the slaves. The Underground Railroad administrators used the expression, "Under the protection of the British Lion," when they were speaking about slaves who safely made their way to Canada. The "British Lion" figures prominently in many African American genealogies because it was a safe haven for those escaping and longing for freedom, long before Americans fought in the Civil War. But especially in the last couple of years before the Civil War, the Underground Railroad was funneling many a happy black man into the welcome arms of host families and employers in Canada. Women and children also made their way to Canada, but their numbers were much fewer.

During the early 1800's, thousands of emigrants from Scotland and Ireland were encouraged by the British to go to Canada. Once there, many Irish women struck up romances with black freedmen. (Few black women made it safely to Canada. There were many more men.) These black men and Irish women enjoyed romantic relationships. And of course there were relationships between black women and Irish men but much fewer. It is not uncommon for black families to have Irish names. Historians speculate on this. Could it be that black men eager to rid themselves of their slavery surname took their Irish wife's surname? Or were the children of these relationships born out of wedlock so took the mother's name? There is plenty of speculation and it is easy to find discussions on this topic on the Internet.

As the shores of North America brought more and more ships of immigrants and slaves, our family trees started to flower. And because they were in the same "class system," poor British immigrants intermingled with the slaves. I hate saying "class system," but that's how I read it when doing research. That's how many people see it. Good luck looking down your nose at other's family tree, that's certainly no fun. Everybody's got a prostitute, pirate or slave somewhere along the line. From what I've read, North America was pretty wild. Canada had its French explorers, trappers and traders. Then the Scots-Irish and the Irish came in. Natives (Canadian Indians) intermarried so frequently with the Colonial French, it's hard to distinguish them from one another in the family trees. After the British reclaimed Acadia in 1710, and renamed it Nova Scotia, there was intermarrying there too. And earlier, after the Brits rustled New Amsterdam out of the hands of the Dutch, and christened it New York, the two groups intermarried even though they had been at war together.

Our dear ancestors had ways in which they enjoyed life and found comfort in one another. Within this crowd were the makings of America. Admixing brought opportunities to share cultures. Including music. Imagine the gatherings. French Canadian fiddle players teaching the youngsters. African banjo players sitting around the campfire late at night. Native American and Metis ethnic foods. Irish girls dancing. They were a colorful, cultural mix of early Americana. Our folk music bears witness to their intermixing. Can we not feel the emotion of the slave and the indentured servant when we hear American folk music? Their longing for freedom from oppression should send shivers.

Indigenous people had been here for thousands of years. Some were not friendly to the Europeans and things grew worse. Some were friendly to the Europeans and were taken advantage of and things still grew worse. Indigenous people were enslaved. Many were sent to Caribbean Islands to work the plantations of sugar cane and rice. There, they coupled with Africans. When they or their descendants made it back to America, they became part of the melting pot. And believe it or not, when given the opportunity, some of them owned slaves as well. And fathered children with their female slaves.

Quote

"Some indigenous South Africans were taken as slaves by the colonists… Though colonial law discriminated against native Africans, a good amount of intermixing occurred between the white settlers and black slaves, resulting in modern Afrikaners with almost 7% of their genes originating from Africa (Thompson, 2014)."

"Estimating Ancestry in South Africa: A Comparison of Geometric Morphometrics and Traditional Craniometrics," page 15, by Rebecca Elizabeth King.

"While all modern populations have undergone genetic evolution in the years since European colonization," Rebecca King states, "the American and South African populations may have changed at a more similar rate…"

Might we therefore think that a similar 7% could be the circumstance for *some* white people whose ancestors were in the South for four-hundred years?

Chapter Two

Breaking Through Old Prejudices

For generations (due to laws like the one-drop rule) anyone with the slightest portion of African ancestry, was labeled as black and subjected to slavery and oppression. If there were any drops of black blood, families kept it a secret. That's why finding black ancestry within a white family is next to impossible. You have to look and look and look. Like archeologists who take toothbrushes and painstakingly sweep soil from tiny bone fragments, we do the same. Just as every bone fragment is priceless, every clue is invaluable. Even if we don't find the answer, someone fifty years from now will have access to previously unreleased documents and they might finally piece it all together. DNA will help facilitate that.

In my search to find connections between whites and blacks with the same surname, I'd be lying if I said I didn't run into opposition. Honestly, I ran into what felt like hostility. My husband and I flew to New Orleans and rented a motorcycle and rode through Louisiana and Mississippi. Armed with computer print-outs and my own genealogical notes, we tooled around on a rented Harley and my patient and adept husband helped me find the rural area where my ancestors lived during the Antebellum era. At the time, I was knee-deep in my fascination with hidden Jewish ancestry. Well… some people are prejudice against blacks *and* Jews and here I was, coming from California wanting to dig up anything and everything I could about my family history. I had questions. Were they Crypto-Jews who owned slaves? Did they have any African blood? Who were my Southern ancestors?

After we returned home and I pondered the reactions I received from those I let in on my genealogical ambitions, my husband was amused and laughed at my innocent, naive thinking. No one threw a pie in my face but looking back, it sometimes feels like it. I thought I had made new connections with distant relatives but they will not respond to my letters or emails and my Southern cousins with whom I had been close, appear to have cut me off. Maybe they're just busy… I doubt it. It's been five years. So I feel I do need to warn you… you might lose a few friends or relatives.

Prejudices that exist in the rural South, are remnants of emotions that ran through the hearts and minds of Southerners after the Civil War, when blacks were freed.

Southern whites were terrified about the change. And freed slaves were misled into believing that after the war, they would be compensated for helping the Yankees win and that they would receive forty-acres and a mule. We all know that never happened. What did happen was some of the Southern farmers got together and started meeting in barns to discuss the new era of Reconstruction and the Ku Klux Klan was born.

If you run across push back when you're conducting a genuine search of your origins, just move on to the next thing on your list. Times are changing and as I'm sure you know, there are thousands of people *in the South*, at universities and genealogical societies who are kind and will lend a hand.

Chapter Three
The Oxford Study

In 2015, Oxford University compared the genes of North and South-Americans with Africans and Europeans. They call the African and European genes the "donors" and the American genes (both north and south) "recipients." Why? Because they were looking for the ancestors of those who populated the Americas.

The researchers were surprised at the genetic complexity. Among American Latinos, the majority of their European genes are Spanish. No secret there. For African Americans (including those from Barbados) the majority of the European genes come from Great Britain. That surprises me. I would have thought French, Spanish, Portuguese and/or Dutch.

This brings us to the Basque of France and Spain. (The ethnic group with the highest rate of Rh-negative blood.) Their contribution to the American genetic make-up is small but "distinct." Their genetic contribution is found in South Americans and Mexico's Mayan people. This is not to say that all South Americans and Mayan have Basque ancestry, but the researchers found the Basque genes in that Latin group. For those of us with Rh-negative blood, this gives us something to ponder.

The Oxford study found that Puerto Rico and the Dominican Republic are closely related genetically and different than the other ethnic groups. The reason for this, the researchers assume, is that the migration patterns between the Caribbean Islands and the American continent were different. And Caribbean populations like Barbados, carry more of an African genetic make-up than those from South America. That should come as no surprise to anyone. Although slavery was prevalent in South America, native people who were already there were taken into slavery. Whereas in the Caribbean Islands, slave traders built huge agricultural plantations and populated them with slaves from Africa.

The study found that the largest percentage of genetic make-up of African Americans today, comes from West Africa, the Yoruba people. (See Chapter Six for another study that differs.) My old Webster's dictionary defines Yoruba as "a Negro of an extensive, linguistic family of the West African coast, mainly between Dahomey and the Niger; also, their language." They are called *Yorubans*. Those from Dahomey are called Dahomans. In the past, Dahomey was a French West African colony. It appears to be independent today. Niger is a river in West Africa.

Quote

Dahomey – [Former] French overseas territory in southeastern [formerly] French West Africa. With an area of about 45,000 square miles, it lies between Nigeria and French Tagoland, stretching from the Gulf of Guinea north to the Niger River. The 70-mile coast contains the ports of Porto Novo, the capital, Ouidah, Cotonou, and Grand Popo. The chief exports, including palm kernels and oil, cacao, coffee, peanuts, cotton, and copra, come mainly from the more fertile Lower Dahomey, while stock raising is more important in the highlands to the north. Industries include vegetable oil extracting and cotton ginning. **Grolier Encyclopedia, volumes 7 & 8, pg 3**.

If you're looking to visit the land of your Dahoman ancestors, it is now located in the country of *Benin*. The African kingdom of Dahomey was in existence between approximately 1600 to 1894. After 1894, it became a French West African colony. In the early 1600's, the Dahomans amassed tremendous power when they conquered strategic cities along the African Atlantic. Those who ruled Dahomey, traded heavily with the Europeans, especially slave traders. Dahomey is known for its noteworthy art, practicing Vodun (Voodoo), and their female military unit, the Dahomey Amazons.

Back to the Oxford study and the Americas. When looked at percentage wise, African genetic make-up varies across the continent (North and South America). The Mayans have "virtually zero" African ancestry, whereas today's Barbadians have 87%. Again, not to say that everyone from Barbados is 87% of African descent, or that there are no Mayan's with African ancestry. These findings come from a careful Oxford study but it doesn't include whole populations. The researchers found that everyone's genetic European versus African make-up varies widely, even within each group. But their findings can help those who have taken DNA tests and seek further knowledge.

The Oxford researchers found Italian genes (Southern Italy and Sicily specifically) among Colombians and Puerto Ricans. They attributed this to the Italian emigrants who came to the Americas in the late 1800's and early 1900's. A similar parallel was found between African Americans with

16

French genetics and the French emigrants who populated places like Louisiana.

"We can see the huge genetic impact that the slave trade had on American populations and our data match historical records," said study author Dr. Garrett Hellenthal from the UCL Genetics Institute. "The majority of African Americans have ancestry similar to the Yoruba people in West Africa, confirming that most African slaves came from this region. In areas of the Americas historically under Spanish rule, populations also have ancestry related to what is now Senegal and Gambia. Records show that around a third of the slaves sent to Spanish America in the 17th Century came from this region, and we can see the genetic evidence of this in modern Americans really clearly."

To read the article in its entirety, search online for: "Complex genetic ancestry of North and South Americans uncovered," by Oxford University.

Chapter Four
The Dutch and their Slaves

Before slavery swept the world, the first African Americans came to the colonies as Indentured Servants. In the early colony of Virginia, they were comfortable intermarrying with Native Americans. The Portuguese, who in early years made their way to the Appalachian Mountains, were also comfortable intermarrying with Africans and Natives. Medieval Spanish women took African men as lovers and husbands. Back then, the world had a history of slavery that knew no color barriers. The word slave derives from the word *Slavic*. The Slavic people were not black.

If your family tree goes back to the colonial era, your ancestors may have had dealings with the Dutch and the Jews... or Dutch Jews. In the early 1600's, the Dutch established trading colonies in Indonesia financed by the East India Company. Dutch men without women were provided prostitutes from the company's slave population, resulting in countless children. I don't know how one could find their Dutch patriarchal line, unless these relationships became legal marriages, (which I'm sure there were plenty) and the surname continued and lives on today. I've got an old globe sitting on my desk where I can trace the routes of the Dutch in their ships. They took slaves from Africa and they also captured them from the ancient islands of Indonesia. The Dutch were very powerful in Java. They went into uncharted areas and built massive plantations. If you've read any of my previous *Secret Genealogy* books, you'll understand that many of the Dutch aristocrats were Crypto-Jews, or Jews who under duress, converted to Christianity. If you have your DNA tested and you have some Jewish ancestral lines, it could come from a variety of scenarios. Don't rule out this Indonesia connection.

Before going to Holland, the Dutch Crypto-Jews had been in Spain and Portugal. They were driven out during the Inquisition. There are records of Jewish Portuguese traders and the history of their adventures is fascinating. There are thousands of surnames in the lists of Inquisitional Jews. You should look through the names to see if any surnames similar to your ancestors are on the list. You might be surprised. There are two lists that I am aware of. Here are the links:

http://my.ynet.co.il/pic/news/nombres.pdf

http://www.datachaco.com/noticias/view/34057?fb_action_ ids=826352030764764&fb_action_types=og.comments&fb _source=other_multiline&action_object_map=%5B147432 3539449461%5D&action_type_map=%5B%22og.commen ts%22%5D&action_ref_map=%5B%5D

The Dutch rationalized their slave trafficking by invoking the Biblical reference of Genesis, Chapter Nine:

25 *And he said, Cursed be Canaan; a servant of servants shall he be unto his brethren.*
26 *And he said, Blessed be the Lord God of Shem; and Canaan shall be his servant.*
27 *God shall enlarge Japheth and he shall dwell in the tents of Shem; and Canaan shall be his servant.*

Quote

"... based on Noah's cursing of Ham's son, Canaan, for pointing his two other brothers, Shem and Japheth, to the nudity of their drunken father (Genesis 9:25-27). Picardt argued that the Hamites (Negroes) had been cursed and sentenced to perpetual servitude under the Shemites (identified with the Jews) and Japhethites (identified with the Europeans). Though the exact origins of this argument are unknown, it would serve as the most important biblical justification for the enslavement of blacks until the nineteenth-century emancipation..."

The Dutch and the East India Company had laws. One such set of laws was *The Statutes of Batavia*. The statutes stated that well-meaning Christians were not to sell to those outside Christendom, meaning no sales to Dutch Sephardic Jews. They called the Jews "unbelievers" and they were not permitted to hold the title of a slave that had been purchased from a Christian. However, the Jews were permitted to sell slaves *to* Christians, allowing many Sephardim to prosper as agents of slavery.

The growth of the slave trade culminated in the capture and enslavement of hundreds of thousands of people. Some

21

sources say well over a million. Natives were captured from the Dutch colony of Batavia and slaves were captured from the many clans and tribes throughout the coasts of Africa and inland Africa. There were slaves from the West Indies and the island of Hispaniola. And the Dutch captured natives from the Atlantic region.

Before the Civil War, slave owners brought their servants to church where they were submitted to sermons extolling the virtues of obeying their masters. In August of 1855, with the help of the Underground Railroad, a former slave reached freedom in Canada. When he wrote back to those who helped him find freedom, he refers to Canada as the "Northern Canaan," meaning he believed he had found the "Promised Land." When I hear something like this, I think of the ancient Hebrews.

When the Dutch arrived along the Hudson, today's Manhattan, someone wrote that it was a "terrestrial Canaan." America was built on a very strong Judaea Christian foundation… the Canaan obsession is a small reminder. Behind me is a stack of music books. I could rummage through the songs, both new and old and find many references to Canaan

In 1677, Dutch theologian Herman Witsius wrote the following; "Great sins of the parents have to be redeemed by a long succession of children and grandchildren, for Canaan and his descendants have been assigned to the Semites and the children of Japheth as slaves."

First, we have to understand who the Canaanites were. Geographically, Canaan is situated in the Middle East and surrounded by the Dead Sea, the Mediterranean Sea and the Sea of Galilee. The Ancient Israelites had a prophecy that Canaan was the land of milk and honey and that God promised it to them for "life everlasting."

Canaan was Noah's grandson and the patriarch of the Canaanites. The Canaanites of the north separated themselves from the Canaanites of Israel and became the powerful nation of Phoenicia. They worshiped what Moses called idols, including a sun god they called Baal and a moon goddess they called Ashtoreth or Astarte. They had decadent religious ceremonies that included sacrificing children. What's known as Canaan was Western Palestine, a geographical area surrounded by the Dead Sea, the Mediterranean Sea and the Sea of Galilee. Moses instructed the Israelites to remove all the Canaanites (Phoenicians) from Palestine (Canaan) because they worshiped idols and he feared they would lead the Israelites astray.

The Biblical figure Abraham was the patriarch of the Israelites. (And the Mohammadeans.) Abraham's grandson Jacob became prosperous and around 1800 B.C.E., he ruled over a portion of Canaan territory. He gave himself a new name, the translation of which is *Israel*. Are you following? Canaan… Jacob… Israel…

Canaan (Kenaan in Hebrew, pronounced Ka-nan/Kan-yan) was the land of milk and honey for the ancient Israelites. It was promised to "them" through biblical prophecy. The English dictionary defines "ken" as a verb meaning "to recognize, discern or admit." "Ken" also refers to "Scots Law" meaning "to recognize as heir" and "kin" means "race, people, clan, tribe or group of people having the same ancestry," making one wonder if "ken/kin" is associated with the promised land of Kenaan and the ancient tribe of Israel, those of who belong, or were "admitted" or "recognized" were "kin." In Hebrew, to say "yes," is to say, "ken."

It was over three-thousand-years-ago above the River Jordan that Moses looked down upon the promised land of Canaan

(Kenaan). The exact geographic location of ancient Canaan is not easy to explain but it corresponds vaguely to the area that was called Palestine before the state of Israel was born. Canaan was the Israelites' "Land of Milk and Honey" which they believed was their destiny through a Biblical prophecy. Moses led the Israelites out of Egypt but he never made it to the "Promised Land" of Canaan but to a hill overlooking it. The Israelites leaving Egypt is called the "Exodus." Joshua assisted Moses in the wilderness and took over as the leader of the Israelites when Moses died. Joshua led the Israelites across the River Jordan after Moses died.

Let's not get Joshua confused with Jacob. All the *Twelve Tribes of Israel* are the descendants of Jacob who ruled over a portion of Canaan territory around 1800 B.C.E. Today "Jews" is used when speaking of "Israelites." Jews are also Semites. Many a "Dutchman" was a Crypto-Jew and like many ethnicities, they owned slaves.

Chapter Five

The Fever Over Rh-negative Blood Type

This chapter will be easier to read if you've read my other *Secret Genealogy* books. I also have a blog where I make frequent posts on Rh-negative blood type. Those of us with this blood type are curious of its origins. This chapter furthers that exploration.

We inherit our blood type from our parents. According to the American Red Cross, the majority of African Americans (forty-seven percent) have O positive blood type. So do the Caucasians (thirty-seven percent), Hispanics (fifty-three percent) and Asians (thirty-nine percent).

Antigens are substances in our blood that can produce an immune response if they are foreign to the body. They are capable of creating an immune system attack on transfused blood if it is foreign. This is why very careful science is enlisted in the blood transfusion process. The eight **common** blood types are differentiated by the presence or lack of specific antigens. There are four **major** blood groups; A, B, AB and O. Two antigens on the surface of our red blood cells are labeled as A and B. **There is a third antigen and it is**

called the Rh factor. If it is present it is labeled as *positive*. If it is absent it is labeled as *negative*.

Some scientists tell us that Rh-negative blood factor began as a mutation well over 25,000 years ago. Let's line up the ethnic groups who have high percentages of their population who carry Rh-negative.

Basque
Oriental Jews of Israel
Black Cochin Jews
Samaritans
Moroccan Berbers

Bearing in mind that the Basque language probably originated in ancient Iberia (Spain), the above ethnic groups lead us to Africa and the Middle East. Evidence of the earliest humans is found in Africa. Later they migrated into the Middle East. Sometimes we like a little evidence and those with Rh-negative blood who struggle to make ancestral connections can at least see options for the paths their ancestors took. If it's believed that Rh-negative blood is a mutation (like blonde hair and blue eyes), having it while a sibling does not, is no different from one sibling having brown hair while the other has blonde.

The men of the Basque provinces are stern and uncompromising; they are devoutly religious. That is a direct quote from an old encyclopedia. It's stereotyping and not politically correct. We don't do that, or we try not to. Stern, uncompromising, devoutly religious… anyone you know? It describes many people of different ethnicities and it is not an exclusive trait of men. But that said, if you're Rh-negative, the highest rates of Rh-negative blood occur in the Basque populations of France and Spain. Close to two-thirds of the Basque population carry one of the (r) negative genes.

These "stern" Basque men, may have been our ancestors. What the encyclopedia has to say about their language is even more intriguing. It says that the Basque language has **no relationship to any other European language**, including that of Spain and France, where their homeland is today. The researcher wrote that, "It is commonly thought that Basque is derived from the language of the ancient Iberians." If you are Rh-negative, the next time you're required to check mark a box for ethnicity, select "other" and write… *Ancient Iberian.* (I'm kidding.)

I have a blog and I sometimes write about the rare Rh-negative blood type. Sometimes I get questions. Here's an example: *I am African American. I have 12 brothers and sisters. I am the only one with the blood type. It confuses me. I know I am different from them all.*

The blog site shows me what people typed into the search engine that led them to my post. Many wonder if Rh-negative blood type signifies Jewish ancestry. Rh-negative is not common in the Jewish population, except for a small population of Jews in Iran who were there when it was called Persia and probably before. It's a funny thing, this blood type. It's found in North Africa (think Berbers and Morocco) and of course, it's very strong in the Basque regions of Spain and France.

I got my dusty old globe out and put my finger on Morocco and spun it around. It's easy to see how the ships that carried immigrants and slaves to the New World from Europe, sailed to Florida and New England, bringing this unusual blood type onto America's shores. The mystery is in wondering who these ancestors were that gave us this blood type. It could have been a Persian- Jewish slave trader during the

1600's who took liberties with his female slaves. It could've been a desert-roaming Bedouin of the Berber tribe who went with the Muslims when they conquered Spain in 711 A.D. It could've been someone from the Basque population, the people whose language and this rare blood type conjure up unusual theories about who they are and where they came from. Or it could come from an ancestor who was a nomadic trader, long ago, traveling the spice route, having a love affair with a woman from one of the above mentioned groups.

Get a world map out and put your finger on Morocco. Run it to the left and you will wind up in the southern reaches of America. Run it a little north and you'll reach Spain and France and the Basque region. Run it to the east and you'll reach Iran, where long ago, small groups of Jews made their homes and perhaps their descendants are still there today. Which brings up another question. Who were these ancient Iranian Jews and why were they in Persia?

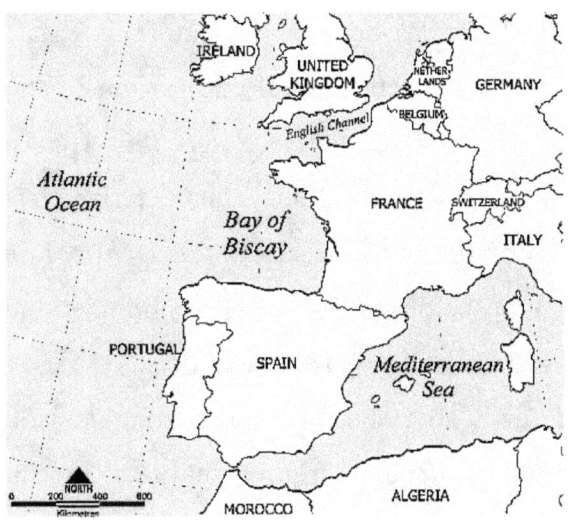

Boise State University student, Michael Davis, did his thesis on the DNA diversity of Basque immigrants. "The Basques are an ancient people, considered by many anthropologists to represent the oldest extant European population," he writes. "Basque populations are characterized by the relatively high frequency of Rh-negative blood types, among the highest in Europe... the Basque became one of the most thoroughly studied populations in Europe, hypothesized to be a genetically isolated remnant of an ancient population."

It is because of this oddity that those of us with Rh-negative blood type are more than curious about our origins. Davis concludes that the evidence, "does not support genetic isolation," of the Basque people but finds that "there is evidence for an ancient (Paleolithic) origin of the Basque ancestors." The keyword here is *Paleolithic*. This is the term for early humans whose culture is characterized by rough or chipped stone implements. Both Neanderthal and Cro-Magnon man belonged to the Paleolithic culture. Cro-Magnon man was tall, erect and regarded as the same species as modern man. But what I garnered from Davis's thesis is that theories of Basque origins linking them to modern Africans or Asians, Ancient Egyptians, **or** Neanderthals have been dispelled.

An Oxford University study found that long **before** the "Vikings" descended on Britain, (between 4,000 and 5,000 B.C.E.) *Iberian* fishermen from coastal Spain migrated through the Bay of Biscay into Britain. DNA from today's British compared with that from the ancient Iberian fishermen reveal that they are practically the same. Bear in mind though that there were a few thousand people already living in Britain at the time the Iberians arrived.

The Basque are the people to whom the Irish are the most closely related genetically. You can include some of the English as sharing the Basque genetics and the Scottish as well. Because there has been less admixture among those living in Ireland, the genetics have remained stable for thousands of years. For those who wonder why they have Rh-negative blood, their research usually leads them to the Basque. Due to their high percentage of Rh-negative (two-thirds of their population) that may be the answer to who your ancestors were. Some people go so far as to say that many Brits; English, Welsh, Scottish and Irish are practically "blood brothers" with the Basque.

If your ancestors inhabited Ireland *before* the English conquered it in 1169, you are much more likely to be descended from the Iberian fishermen. Possibly even a direct descendant. Traditional Irish surnames play prominently in distinguishing those with the Iberian connection.

Old Irish Gaelic surnames:
http://www.rootsweb.ancestry.com/~irlkik/ihm/irenames.htm

For an extensive list of Scottish Gaelic surnames:
http://www.clanscottsociety.org/linked/MostCommonScottishSurnames.html

Let me repeat. The Basque are an uncommon people. Their language has no relationship to any other European language, including that of Spain and France, where the Basque homeland is today. And as I mentioned before, researchers believe that the Basque language is derived from the language of the ancient *Iberians*.

My old dictionary has this entry for **Iberian race:**
A member of the Iberian race (of which the Spanish Iberians are typical), a short, dark, dolichocephalic race, probably the neolithic inhabitants of western Europe. One of an ancient people of the Caucasus, probably ancestors of the modern Georgians. A native or inhabitant of Spain or Portugal.

Dolichocephalic means, "long headed" or "long cranium." Many African Americans are dolichocephalic. I ran across a discussion on ForumBiodiversity.com. Someone asked which nations had the most dolichocephalic skulls. I can't prove that the answers are accurate but they are interesting:

1.) Most dolichocephalic in Europe: Spain/Portugal

2.) The book Anthropologia suecica from the beginning of the 1900s showed that 30% of all Swedes were dolicocephalic...

3.) Most dolichocephalic, probably Mali? I am not too sure on this one.

4.) Dolichocephalic- Senegal

The first answer of Spain and Portugal gives us a geographical area near the Basque homelands. The Moroccan Berbers were also nearby. Scottish history tells me that the Scots were largely dolichocephalic. The Swedes were part of the Viking invasions so they could have brought dolicocephalic heads to Scotland. Iberians also inhabited Ireland. Mali and Senegal are in northwestern Africa and so that fits. Senegal runs along the coast and that is where invading ships came to kidnap the indigenous people for the slave trade.

An American with Rh-negative blood and a dolichocephalic head could very well be a descendant of an ancient tribe that migrated from the northwest coast of Africa to northern Africa, up through the Iberian Peninsula and then to

35

Scotland. This is just one scenario. There are many that one can conjure.

Another scenario for those of us with Rh-negative blood, could be that we have an Arabic ancestor from the *Tuareg* tribe of nomads. The Tuaregs are Berbers, dominant in the central and western Sahara. They preserve their *Hamitic* speech but they're Muslim. The Arabic is *Tawariq*, which is the plural of *Tariq*.

In the eleventh century the Tuaregs were ruthless slavers. How many natives from the Upper Niger were sold, no one can know for sure. But by 1880, a Sultan remains in the history books for building an empire by capturing natives and selling them to the Tuaregs, in excess of a *million* and maybe as high as a *million-and-a-half* slaves. Elephants were slaughtered for their white ivory and slaves were enlisted to carry the large tusks on their shoulders. *Black Ivory*, the slaves were called.

Let's get back to the ancient Persian Jews who have a high rate of Rh-negative blood. According to Wikipedia, Jews have lived in what today constitutes Iran, for over 2,700 years. References to their life in Persia (Iran today) are written about in the Bible in Isaiah, Daniel, Ezra and Nehemiah. "Jews who migrated to ancient Persia mostly lived in their own communities. The Persian Jewish communities include the ancient… communities not only of Iran, but also the Armenian, Georgian, Iraqi, Bukharan, and Mountain Jewish communities… Some of the communities were isolated from other Jewish communities, to the extent that their classification as 'Persian Jews' is a matter of linguistic or geographical convenience rather than actual historical relationship with one another. During the peak of the Persian Empire, Jews are thought to have comprised as much as 20% of the population… Jews trace their heritage in Iran to the Babylonian Exile of the 6th century BC and have retained their ethnic, linguistic, and religious identity."

Wikipedia further states that the Jewish community in the Caucasus country of Georgia, is ancient. "The Georgian Jews were considered ethnically and culturally distinct from neighboring Mountain Jews. They were also traditionally a highly separate group to the Ashkenazi Jews in Georgia, who arrived following the Russian annexation of Georgia… As a result of a major emigration wave in the 1990's, the vast majority of Georgian Jews now live in Israel."

Georgia is an Eastern European country but it's almost in Asia. It sits between two Caucasus mountain ranges and butts up to the Black Sea in the western part of the country. It borders Russia in the north and northeast. Georgia's southern neighbors are Turkey and Armenia and Azerbaijan in the southeast.

According to Wikipedia, there were a number of ancient sovereign kingdoms that arose in the area of what is now Georgia. The two most important being *Colchis* in the west and *Iberia* in the east. (This is not to be confused with Iberia/Spain/Portugal but it does seem they might be connected.) They became Christian kingdoms in the 4th century. "… a unified Kingdom of Georgia reached the peak of its political and economic strength during the reign of King David IV and Queen Tamar from the 11th to 13th centuries. In the early modern period, Georgia became fractured and fell into decline due to the onslaught of various hostile empires, including the Mongols, the Ottoman Empire, and Persia. In 1783, Eastern Georgia forged an alliance with the Russian Empire, which led to the gradual annexation of Georgia by Russia starting in 1801."

Looking again at Wikipedia, they state that the "Principality of Iberia and Principate of Iberia... are conventional terms to describe an early medieval aristocratic regime in Caucasian Georgia..." flourishing "between the sixth and ninth centuries, when the leading political authority was exercised by a succession of princes." There was a "core region in what is now central and eastern Georgia known as Kartli to the natives and as *Iberia* to Classical and Byzantine authors. Its borders fluctuated greatly as the presiding princes of Iberia confronted the Persians, Byzantines, Khazars, Arabs, and the neighboring Caucasian rulers throughout this period." More research needs to be done asking the question... what is the connection between this *Iberia* and the *Iberia* associated with Spain?

To those of you who worry about having this odd blood type (Rh-negative), and your siblings don't, you needn't worry. We inherit differently than our siblings. If your blood type is different than theirs, it doesn't mean that you have different parents. I don't believe my brother and sister have Rh-negative, just me. And I never knew my parent's blood type but my mother always said we were related to William the Conqueror. Back in 1066, he was the first "Norman" king of England. "Norman" means a man from the north, called this because his ancestors were Vikings from the north. History shows that some of the royals in this line had the odd blood type Rh-negative. If you carry this blood type, you could be a descendant of British royalty. There is no end to the scenarios one can formulate.

Quote

The people of Gascony, like those of Britanny, possess marked characteristics which distinguish them from other Frenchmen. Gascons are not pure French. In the northern part of the Iberian Peninsula, which occupies both slopes of the Pyrenees, live the remains of a very ancient people who were called Vascones in ancient times. They were mountaineers, herdsmen and shepherds, and although they were assailed by Cathaginians, Romans, Saracens, Goths, French and Spaniards, they have preserved their race identity to the present day, together with the most remarkable language in Europe, and customs which differ from those of all neighboring people. They are commonly known as Basques, but those who lived on the northern slope of the Pyrenees absorbed a portion of the great Gothic invasion, and the Vascones became known as Gascons within the border of France. They are to France what the Highlanders are to Scotland — bold, impetuous and untamable by

40

oppression, but good citizens and splendid soldiers when allowed their own ways. Their physical characteristics are a medium build, somewhat spare but extremely robust and possessed of great activity. They are the darkest skinned people of France, and have large gray eyes and black hair. They have been, and still are, blustering fellows with the strutting ways of the game cock, and with the same appetite for battle. Gasconade is a synonym for brag, bluff, or a blustering manner. They are extremely democratic in their ideas, and the few titled people among them obtained their honors for participating in the wars with the Moors."

"Landmarks of Detroit, a History of the City," by Robert B. Ross and George B. Catlin.

Do an Internet search and look up the flag for the **country** of Georgia. It is almost identical to the flag of the Christian Crusades. And although Georgia became a Christian kingdom in the 4th century, King David IV and Queen Tamar who reigned from the 11th to the 13th give us a clue to their ancient heritage. David and Tamar are Jewish names.

Because Berbers play a role in the maybe ancestry of those of us with Rh-negative blood, it's worth noting that they played no small role in world politics during medieval times.

They are a Mediterranean-type people who inhabit Africa, north of the Sahara. Their descendants historically spread throughout southern and western Europe and today, like many other ethnicities, they are found throughout the world, including North America.

The Berbers are recorded as being medium in height, long-headed (dolichocephalic) with narrow noses. The majority of Berbers have wavy black hair and dark eyes. It is rare to find blond Berbers but occasionally they are seen in the upper ranges of the Atlas Mountains. The Berbers are culturally different from the Hamites of northeastern Africa and from Arab societies that live under patriarchy. History records Berber society as more socially organized and democratic. Those familiar with them say they are, "straight forward and honest in their dealings and of high intelligence." They are excellent horsemen and courageous fighters. They are a mining and agricultural people, exhibiting exceptional skill in metalworking, leather crafts and pottery.

Grolier encyclopedia states that the Berber name "may be a primitive designation modified in classical times as the Greek *barbaroi* or outsiders." In *The Journal of the Royal*

Asiatic Society of Great Britain and Ireland, they state that the original name for the Berbers (Berebbers) is *Mazirgh*, which means, "free, dominant or noble race," and that Mazirgh was the son of Canaan, grandson of Ham and great-grandson of Noah.

Furthermore, the Asiatic Society's journal (a very old book, dating back to the early 1800's with the most prominent list of members I've ever laid eyes on) states that the first ancestor of the Berbers was *Mazirgh* and his descendant was named Bernas (or Berr). An offspring of Bernas is the Gomera tribe from Yemen. The Gomerah (different spelling but same tribe) dwell in the ancient provinces of Er-Riff and Ghart, not far from the Mediterranean, "near the Spanish settlement of Pennon de Velez, where there is a mountain, a river, and a large village, all known by the name of Gomera. An English geographer, EMMANUEL BOWEN, has thought he could prove that these Gomerah are descended from Gomer, the eldest son of JAPET, and that they were one and the same race with the Cimbri, the Celts, and the Eusks, or Cantabrians, in Europe. It has always been supposed that the last-mentioned people were of an African origin…"

Mazirgh, Bernas, Gomerah… these names remind me of Gaelic surnames.

Quote

Analysis of the marrow of the most ancient Egyptian skeletons suggests similarity with the blood of the Haratin, a population in the Algerian desert. (Van Sertima, p. 68). They are called black Berbers, and are descended from an ancient population that lived in the Sahara before it dried out and became a desert. The ancient Egyptians are more closely related to other Africans than to any group outside of Africa and especially to the people living south of Egypt in the Nile valley and Ethiopia today. http://crab.rutgers.edu/~glasker/DIFFERENTAFRICANS2 003.htm

Chapter Six

Getting a Little Teeth Into It

If you remove the color of someone's skin, can you tell what ethnicity they are? People come in all different shapes, sizes, bone structures, etc. There is a huge diversity within us all, even when we're separated into groups or "races." I love to look for similarities between people. Maybe it's my way of connecting to the world. Perhaps it comes from a need to *not* feel alienated. Studies show that most of us feel alienated from time to time, advertisers prey on that particular human vulnerability.

So let's get down to the teeth of it. I have a new word in my vocabulary... dentition. It has to do with the development of teeth, the number, kind and arrangement.

In 2002, completing her doctorate in anthropology at Ohio State University, Heather Joy Hecht Edgar was interested in teeth. Just in case you're about to roll your eyes, her research was supported by the National Science Foundation and the American Museum of Natural History. She also received a grant from the university. She set out to prove her hypothesis that during the last 400 years, the genetically determined structure of the teeth of African Americans, lies somewhere in the middle, between Western Europeans and West Africans. The research was also done to help identify human remains. If there are any differences in the teeth between European Americans and African Americans, it helps forensic scientists identify deceased bodies. This gets confusing so stay with me. Don't get *Western Europeans* confused with *European Americans* and don't confuse *West Africans* with *African Americans*.

Skeletons were gathered from reputable sources and their teeth were studied. The conclusion was that modern African Americans have genetically changed since their first contact in the American colonies. Over the years, they have lost their strong genetic African traits and acquired some European traits, so today, they fall somewhere in between Western Europeans and West Africans. We didn't need a doctoral candidate to tell us this but if anyone wants to argue about it, we have a respectable source.

Researchers studied skeletal remains representing the days of America's early colonies and compared them throughout the last 400 years, this included modern skeletons. Over time, African Americans have become less like their West African ancestors. Again, they fall somewhere in the middle between their original ancestors and that of their new ancestors, those of their new land, America. The proof is in the teeth.

The author of the study, Heather Edgar expected other findings. She set out to show that after the Civil War, European genetic "flow" decreased. In other words, after the Civil War, white plantation owners no longer had slaves that they could abuse. The results of the study were mixed. Even though more genetic change occurred in the early colonial years, the progression of African Americans toward the middle was "progressive over time."

History shows that darker-skinned African Americans were more likely to stay in the south, than those with lighter skin who found their way to the urban areas of the north. By looking at the teeth of the deceased, they have concluded this to be correct. African Americans in the south, whether they're from the country or the city, are similar in their genetics. Whereas, if you compare the dental specimens between a rural African American who lives in Louisiana and an African American who lives in Chicago, they show much greater genetic distance.

When the teeth of the European American skeletons (dead white folks) were compared, their strongest similarity was to *rural* African Americans of the South not to African Americans who migrated north. This is not what the researchers expected to find. This points to there being more "admixture" of the genes in African Americans who did *not* migrate out of the rural South. In other words, what the research set out to prove was that once slavery was over, there was a drop in admixture. The researchers were not expecting an increase in admixture. More recent dental samples are needed to study this and come to any conclusion. The study is listed in the bibliography if you would like to read it.

The study found that the dental traits between the African Americans and European Americans were "overwhelming" similar. Only about eleven-and-a-half percent of the traits were different enough to form an opinion which ethnic group the teeth belonged to.

Furthermore, the study found that the Western European teeth are more closely related to the African Americans than to the European Americans. For example, a white man from London would have teeth more like a black man from Louisiana than a white man from Louisiana. Here's why. It has to do with Western Europeans who were "admixing" with their slaves *before* the Civil War. *After* the war, no more slavers and the majority of emigrants to America were from Eastern and Southern Europe. The Eastern and Southern-Europeans came *after* slavery. So the people who are referred to as European Americans has changed. The conclusion is that "the pool of individuals who today are thought of as Americans of European heritage is of a somewhat different heritage than was true in previous generations." An interesting statement to ponder while you're doing your family tree.

And then there are the Gullahs. Who are the Gullahs? They are African Americans from South Carolina. The study says they were from "the outer banks" of Africa. Their genetics have mixed the least with Western Europeans. The teeth of the Gullahs are quite a bit different from West Africans. They are also different from African American teeth samples from all the time periods in the study. This may indicate that the Gullah descend from "particular areas, such as Senegal, Guinea, and Sierra Leone." The Gullah were brought to America because of their knowledge of rice farming. Rice farms were in the "Upper South" so received slaves earlier that the "Lower South" (the area south of North Carolina).

I don't know how these anthropologists keep their heads from spinning off. They're focusing on details that are never going to be precise. All this makes us ask… who were the Southerners who admixed with their slaves? After the Indians were relocated (for more on this read *Secret Genealogy IV – Native Americans in Our Family Trees*) their land was "ceded" and primarily populated by the English. Other ethnicities who populated the "Old South" were the Welsh, Irish, Scots and Germans. There were French protestants, *Huguenots* who populated America's early South, some of who may have been Jewish and hiding their ethnicity to escape persecution.

Chapter Seven

A boarder? A Worker? A Household Slave?

"Free Soil" was the American expression that referred to territories where slavery was outlawed. Before the Civil War, due to the abolitionists desire to have slavery abolished in all the territories, they were particularly concerned with the large swath of land that Mexico seceded in 1848. Crucial voting power was at stake and the Southern states were deeply concerned. If they could not abolish slavery, they believed that they could at least keep it confined to those states where it was legal.

Before the war, for about twenty-five years, as many as 25,000 slaves found refuge in a secret network of safe havens called the *Underground Railroad* or the *Underground Railway*. Organized by Northern abolitionists, kind and brave people along the route assisted escaped Southern slaves. Their destination was Canada. Once across the border, they obtained the *protection of the British Lion,* and became free men and women.

The most well-traveled routes for fugitive slaves was through Ohio and Pennsylvania. Along the route, empathetic people assisted. They fed them, housed them in their barns and hideaways, and even gave them money. Runaway slaves contorted their bodies into unbelievable positions and stayed cramped for hours and often days in shipping containers and any other imaginable box or furniture large enough to hold a human body. Nervous abolitionists posed as masters of fugitive slaves. The two sat on trains together, hoping no one would discover their lies. Creative personas were devised to impersonate Southern plantation owners and new identities were given to the fugitives. Any ideas that would bring freedom to the enslaved was seriously considered. Fortunately, because of the ingenuity of others, many a fugitive slave found his way to Canada.

Abolitionists traveled to the South and sought out slaves. Not all were believed to be strong enough to attempt an escape but if an abolitionist believed a slave looked hearty in mind and spirit, that slave was quizzed. After getting friendly they would ask a question like, "Gee, wouldn't it be nice to be free?" If they received an affirmative response, they could then ask, "Have you heard of the Underground Railroad?" A further question might be, "Did you know that if you make it to Canada you would be free?" Which would prompt another question, "Would you be willing to go if you had a sponsor?"

There were more black men than women who escaped to Canada. These men wanted wives and often found them in the multitude of Irish girls who the British shipped to Canada to populate their colonial territory. (They Brits wanted to out-number the French who they'd expelled from their homelands.) Many freedmen tried in vain to have their enslaved wives join them in Canada. When they were unable to do so, some of them married the Irish girls. It's recorded that in Montreal alone, there were 1,500 "young lady immigrants... in distress... starving and freezing." Might not these young women find comfort in the arms of freedmen fresh upon Canadian lands as well? *These historical people are someone's ancestors.* And it wasn't just Canadian shores that thousands of Irish entered. It's estimated that between 1845 and 1860, fifty percent of American immigrants were

Irish. In Vermont in 1850, the Irish held the record as the largest population of immigrants.

Some slaves refused to go to Canada but instead chose to stay on free American soil. Many angry plantation owners sent bounty hunters after their runaway slaves but they were often met with strong resistance. Armed with swords and guns, slaves fought for their freedom. Their mantra was, "Give me liberty or give me death."

Cities like Boston, Massachusetts; Richmond, Virginia; and Charleston, South Carolina had the train running through. Any of those cities could have passengers hop on board with an abolitionist and a slave, both of whom might be disguising their identities. In 1850, Boston was considered a safe haven for escapees but that did not stop plantation owners from going to great expense to try to retrieve what they considered was their property. And with the Fugitive Slave Law on their side, sometimes their efforts paid off. Unless of course, a newly freed man was willing to fight to the death. Or the crafty network of abolitionists knew that they were coming and took great steps to secure the fugitives.

It wasn't until 1870, when the first census after the Civil War was taken, that African Americans were included by name along with the rest of the population. This census is often the first official record of a surname for former slaves. It lists the person's age and place of birth. For 1880 and later, the census shows the relationships within the family of each household.

Before the war, when the census workers went to a home in a free state, and found a black person living in the home, one has to wonder, with so much abolitionist support, if they didn't fudge and not record someone as black. If a fugitive was mulatto, could an abolitionist convince the census taker that their "boarder" was French? Or Spanish? I ran across an 1860 United States Federal Census. This is not long before the Civil War broke out in 1861. There is an entry: *Moses Dupo 19, born in France*. His name is not the same as the family. Who is he? He could be a boarder, a worker or... a protected slave who had escaped from the south. Because it was Detroit, Pike, Illinois, a northern territory, it should be looked into.

Unusual names that differ from family members listed on a census, are important clues, especially for those looking for black ancestors. My research from here would send me to ask questions about the Underground Railroad and their role in 1860 in Detroit, Pike Illinois. It was a free state. This family could easily be providing a safe haven for this man. He could also have been a family servant or farmhand, he's the right age. Another option is that he could have been purchased by this family, in order to free him. That was done frequently, especially by Northerners. It's not always easy to tell, but what a pity it would be if a family risked their safety to provide freedom for a young man, only to have the genealogical record speak otherwise.

Here's the way the entry looked:

William Morris 26, KY

Martha J Morris 21, IL

Laura E Morris 2, IL

Charles B Morris 10/12, IL

Moses Dupo 19, France

Who is Moses? A boarder? A worker? A household slave? A fugitive slave from the South?

The 1870 census no longer has the young Frenchman, Moses Dupo living with the Morris family. It was after the Civil War so if he was a slave, he would be freed. The US Census lists their Post Office as Detroit. What does it mean to be in Detroit, Illinois between the years 1860 and 1870?

Detroit, Illinois is situated really close to the Missouri border. In 1860, Missouri had thousands of slaves. They worked the tobacco, grain and hemp fields, and handled livestock. Slaves were also enlisted to work on the Mississippi River on the ferries. In 1824, Illinois voted against legal slavery. In 1828, they began the slow process of emancipation. In 1848 Illinois banned slavery. Even still, in 1853 Illinois adopted an anti-Black law which would make it difficult to seek refuge in that state.

The original French spelling for Moses Dupo could be *Dupuis*. What happens when we google *Moses Dupuis*? Not a lot. But when I google *Moses Dupuis Detroit Illinois black*, I find a lot of interesting French Canadian history. And then I get lost in the Metis, French Canadian history that is not my focus. But guess what? I keep digging and no, I did not find out if Moses Dupo was a fugitive slave. I have no idea who he is but I found an excellent source of Metis history with surnames that might fit some other research I've been working on. Well written too. And there were a lot of slaves listed in their French Canadian marriage records. And when

I got lost, I found someone's thoughts on who the Basque people are. It's perfect for the chapter on Rh-negative. It's then that I believe once again in the magic of getting lost.

Here is some helpful information about finding black ancestry on the censuses. It is taken from the National Archives and Records Administration in Washington, DC:

For the years 1790 to 1930, there is a microfilm record of each available census of free and slave populations arranged by state, county, and enumeration division. The Federal Constitution stipulated that a slave counted as three-fifths of a person for purposes of taxation and apportionment of the House of Representatives.

Another census, called "The Federal Population Schedules, 1790–1840," lists only the heads of free households. All others, including slaves, are noted statistically under the head of household or reported owner.

Another census is the "Free African Americans in 1790–1840." The remainder of the free population is numbered. Black (B) or Mulatto (M) indicates the race of the head of the household. Other members of the household were listed in age brackets by sex.

Censuses for 1790 and 1810 list free nonwhites in a category titled "all other free persons;" there is no distinction made between free blacks and Native Americans not on reservations.

The censuses for 1820–1840 listed people of color separately.

Slaves in the 1790–1840 Census: no notation of slave by name, age, sex, or origination appears. The census lists slaves statistically under the owner's name.

Free African Americans in the 1850 and 1860 Censuses. Beginning in 1850, the census named all free members of households, white and nonwhite. The enumerator recorded the person's name, age, sex, place of birth, and the color of each free person in a household (e.g., black, white, or mulatto).

Slaves in the 1850 and 1860 Censuses. For these two censuses, slaves were enumerated on a separate schedule.

The census does not record slave names; census takers were instructed to substitute numbers in place of names on the slave schedules. The slave schedules are arranged by state, then by county, and then by owner. These schedules record the number of slaves owned and their color (black or mulatto); sex; age; whether "deaf, dumb, blind, insane, or idiotic"; the number of fugitives from the state; and the number manumitted. There is no index for the slave schedules.

The Federal Mortality Schedules, 1850–1880, contain the names of persons who died in the 12 months preceding the date of the census. Unlike the Federal population schedules, the Mortality Schedules for 1850 and 1860 often include the names of slaves. These schedules include information such as the decedent's race, marital status, whether free or slave (1850 and 1860), age, and cause of death. The National Archives has a partial collection of Mortality Schedules on microfilm where you can search for the state and county in which the slave died although slave age and place of birth were often estimated, leading to many inaccuracies.

The National Archives also has a "Special List 34." It is a list of Free Black Heads of Families in the First Census of the United States, 1790. Another that is worth looking at is the "Federal Nonpopulation Census Schedules, 1850–1880."

I know that those searching Native American ancestry often go in person to the National Archives research facilities. And Ancestry.com has every census from 1790 to 1930. They are "searchable." I have found them a little hard to read but you can zoom in on them, which helps a lot.

Chapter Eight

Slavery Petitions

In 1991, a project called *The Slavery Petitions* got underway. A group of historians began to "collect, organize, and publish" court petitions from the time period of the American Revolution through the Civil War, from the fifteen former slaveholding states and the District of Columbia. The Slavery Petitions are of great historical importance. The project includes all "accessible petitions written on behalf of or by slaves and on behalf of or by free blacks from the selected counties…" It also includes all "accessible petitions written by slaveholding white women seeking divorce or alimony from the selected counties…"

The slavery petitions are in PDF form and there is a "find" feature, enabling the search of surnames. The information in the slavery petitions gives a researcher the ability to trace slaves who belonged to an estate. Because some of the free blacks were required to have a white guardian, if the name of the guardian is listed, it's possible to trace the destiny of the slaves mentioned in the entries.

There is no way to verify that these slavery petitions are factual, the narratives could have come from angry husbands and wives wishing ill on their spouses. They are eye-openers. There was a lot of promiscuity in 1840 and it's important to understand that there were consensual relationships between white men and black women and black men and white women. And there were children born from these affairs. *Maybe they are our ancestors.*

In 1840, in Guilford County, North Carolina, a man named William King was suspicious of his wife. He was sure that Mary was cheating on him. Mary and her sister were not careful enough and William heard them planning a suspicious evening out. One night, he followed his wife to her mother's house where he found Mary and her sister distracted with two men. William complained that Mary had her head on the lap of a "Mulatto fellow." If Mary left North Carolina and had a baby with the "Mulatto fellow" whose lap she rested her head, the child might very well have been born with the surname King.

There is no way that we can look at census records or family trees and see what color of skin our ancestors had. I'm tremendously curious about my family history. If a branch of my family tree leads to Africa, I want to know.

And how do you sort out your genealogy when your ancestor was accused of being a prostitute? Cordelia Miller's husband Nathan, claimed that after he left to fight in the Civil War, she fell into prostitution and took up with "Yankees" and "Negroes" in Asheville, North Carolina. The war took a toll on the Miller's happy marriage and Cordelia wound up in jail. That's Nathan's story. Who knows. Poor Cordelia can't speak for herself, maybe she was helping the Yankees recuperate. We will never know, but what a great clue it would be, if you are Cordelia or Nathan's descendant.

Cordelia wasn't the only one accused of being a prostitute. In 1828, Zilphia Bishop's husband accused her of that too. His claim was that Zilphia enjoyed the intimacies of a slave named Brister. Cordelia eventually found her way into the arms of another man, a white man, but this fellow, Brister is probably someone's beloved ancestor. We might not know his last name but we could do some investigating in the census records of Craven County, North Carolina and see what we come up with. Maybe there was a Bishop plantation and Brister lived at one of the neighboring farms.

Temperance Flowers's husband Thomas wasn't too happy with her either. He told the court that Temperance had begun associating with people of color and had a child with one of them. Thomas was requesting a divorce, so the baby no doubt was born with the surname Flowers. This is an example of a white woman having a consensual relationship with a black man.

You might think that free white women voluntarily risking an unlawful relationship with a black man was rare, but the Slavery Petitions show us this wasn't the case. There are quite a few stories. There's got to be a record out there for a mulatto baby born in 1829 in Perquimans County, North Carolina. Gabriel Goodwin's mind was blown when the baby was born dark. It's quite possible that baby bore the surname Goodwin, since that was the mother's legal surname. Judging by the entry, that must have been quite a shock to Mr. Goodwin, who assumed his wife was faithful.

Gabriel wasn't the only husband whose mind was blown. A few years before the Civil War, William Hanner fell into great "mortification" when his wife Charlotte gave birth to a black baby. Charlotte didn't stick around. She fled with her new baby.

But William Hickman didn't catch on as quickly. It took him eighteen years to become suspicious that his children were not his biological offspring. And another four years after that before he uncovered the identity of the children's father... a mulatto slave that lived nearby. Hickman seems a pretty patient fellow and considerate of others. Even after knowing that his children were not his offspring, he stayed with his wife for fear of embarrassing her family. I suspect the Hickman children were listed as white on the census and not mulatto, like their biological father. Their descendants might look so white today, no one would even think that their ancestors were African Americans.

And things were not all that calm at the Wake County, North Carolina home of a family named Lee. Elizabeth Lee insisted that her husband Elisha was having a fling with a black woman. In 1828, she was so upset, she left him. Interestingly enough, she gave birth to a mulatto child after she left.

Sounds like Elizabeth was accusing her husband of something she herself was guilty of... adultery. I wonder what surname Elizabeth's baby was given in the hospital. Even if the baby was dark, like Elisha claimed, during that era, I imagine Elizabeth would have insisted her baby was white.

In another story, we learn that Andrew Whittington's wife Lucy, gave birth to two illegitimate children. They could very well have been born black, considering that Andrew saw her in bed with a free black man, Ned Gower. Andrew was so enraged, he called Lucy's behavior with men (white or black) *criminal intercourse*. Back in 1830, that's exactly what it was, criminal. Infidelity was a serious offense... *especially* between black and white lovers.

It sounds like liaisons between whites and blacks wasn't that uncommon in North Carolina back in the early 1800's. Nor were women who liked to drink. Richard Jernigan of Wayne County, blamed the bottle on his wife's lustful desires for men, including men of color. Due to her scandalous behavior, Richard said she gave him venereal disease. She'd also developed a nasty temper. After twenty-five years of marriage, he'd had enough. And Richard's wife wasn't the only one with a bad temper. Anne Wilson claimed that her husband William had one of his slaves beat her. Anne and William were going through a nasty divorce and she wanted custody of the slaves but probably not her husband's black mistress who he was sleeping with in Anne's bed.

Wesley Gray claimed his wife's men friends were not only colored but vile and that she boasted of her liaisons in public. He wasn't alone in his complaints. Andrew Troutman said his wife had taken up with a free black man too, named John Bennet. And Mary Bostian confessed to her husband that she'd been unfaithful and had been sleeping with a black man. She also gave birth to a mulatto child. That was in 1866.

Graham Jones wasn't thrilled either when he married Sina Lincoln (because she was pregnant) and the baby was born mulatto. Graham was white, so apparently Sina wasn't being straight with him, so he wanted a divorce.

And Mary Richardson wanted a divorce from her husband Andrew, who was cohabitating with a free black woman. Is it fair to assume that the free black woman was living with Mary's husband voluntarily? I think so. Although it does surprise me. Not that a black woman can't love a white man, of course she can. But it sounds like there was a lot of sexual liaisons between blacks and whites at a time when it was a major criminal offense. That people would risk severe punishment is a testament to love.

And it happened the other way around too. Martha Fogg was black and her baby was white. The white baby confirmed Mary Williams suspicions that her husband was having an affair with a black woman. And an entry in 1837 about a slave named Sue Ellen, (that's my name) reminds me of my Southern heritage. Fortunately for me, I was born free. Poor Sue Ellen though. She and her two children were part of a probate and put up for sale.

The stories are candid and colorful. Maybe they're not your relatives, but they belong to someone who may be looking to connect these historical figures to their family trees. After reading of such wild infidelity though, it gives a genealogist pause and makes DNA testing attractive for those who long for perfection and not assumptions as to who their ancestors were.

Quote

"The county court petitions in this collection offer immediate testimony on a broad range of subjects by a variety of southerners—black and white, slave and free, slaveholder and nonslaveholder, men and women. The documents include rare biographical and genealogical information about people of color; they detail how slaves, as chattel, could and often did find themselves sold, conveyed, or distributed as part of their masters' estates; and they reveal the impact of market forces on the slave family. The guardianship and emancipation petitions present an unusually clear picture of the association between whites and free blacks, and the divorce petitions provide a unique picture of slaveholding white women."

http://academic.lexisnexis.com/documents/upa_cis/16456_ RSFBSlaveryPetitionsSerIIPt%20D.pdf

The Slavery Petitions has a name index in the back. I looked up the surname of a known slaveholder, *Eliza Holmes*. He is listed. The number next to the name is 11: 0738. He is listed in the name index but when I go to the listing, his name is not listed. But it looks like this is his family:

0738 (Accession # 21382432). Charleston District, South Carolina. **Ann Holmes**, executrix of the estate of her late husband, **John Holmes**, seeks direction from the court in discharging the estate's considerable debts. She has sold the slaves in the estate, which generated $7,032.10, but she reports that the estate is "still in such an embarrassed condition that she [knows] not which of the claims to pay with safety." Her marriage settlement with her husband secured eleven slaves in trust, and Ann informs the court that she has used "one moiety of the crop made by the said negro slaves" for the support and maintenance of herself and her children. The petitioner asks the court to require the various creditors to "interplead and settle and adjust their said demands between themselves." She asserts her willingness to "bring the assetts into this Honorable Court or put them in the hands of a receiver to abide its further order."

Note that there are only two names; Ann and John Holmes. Yet in the name index, there are five other names with the same numbers next to them: Holmes, Amy Helen 11: 0738; Holmes, Ann G. 11: 0738; Holmes, Francis Simmons 11: 0738; Holmes, John Hanscombe 11: 0738 and Holmes, Sarah Harriet 11: 0738.

The year is 1824. Because this Holmes genealogy has been well-researched by my distant Mississippi cousins, I know that these are **not** my Holmes ancestors. But I suspect that there is a connection, because the patriarch of my line, is a John Holmes who has a son named Elisha. But they were in Georgia before they went to Mississippi.

It might be wise to go through all the listings of your surnames you're researching and see what comes up. Even though the entries are North and South Carolina, there may be other states compiled by now and many American families were in the Carolinas *before* they went elsewhere. It is worth looking, especially because you are seeking answers to your multi-ethnic questions. Read and study the entries of your surname and then... sleep on it. You just never know what might come to your mind.

There are thirty-nine Holmes names listed in the name index. Because I know that a Mississippi Holmes plantation had a slave named "Lucy," I looked at this entry: Holmes, Lucy 20: 0568:

0568 (Accession # 21385244). Charleston District, South Carolina. Thomas Drayton Holmes and Isaac McDowell Holmes, a minor, ask for the appointment of a trustee and for an account and distribution of money. In 1827, their grandfather, Thomas Drayton, died having executed a last will and testament. His said will directed that his estate be divided into five parts among his heirs. The petitioners assert that the administrator paid the debts and that the "negro slaves" were "allotted and divided among the Legatees." The petitioners' mother received fifteen slaves, who were "delivered to your Orators father, Henry P Holmes." Henry sold the slaves to Stephen D. Miller for $4,500. Miller entered into a bond for this amount and agreed to pay for the slaves in three parts. Miller later moved with the slaves to Mississippi, where he died "leaving his estate much embarrassed." They assert that the slaves were never paid for and that a sizeable interest has now accrued. They further reveal that their parents have both died and that they and their sister, Henrietta Caroline Holmes Egleston, recently married, are the surviving heirs. Noting that said Henrietta "has recovered a judgment in the State of Mississippi" for a considerable sum of money, Thomas and Isaac Holmes request the appointment of a trustee and their equal share of said money.

Lucy is not mentioned in the entry. It appears that she is the unmentioned sister, and that she is an heir. These are not the Holmes I'm searching for but I hope this example explains how you might use the slavery petitions for your own genealogical search. And as I said, there just might be a connection to my Mississippi Holmes ancestors but I think my time would be better spent on stronger links.

With all this playing around, it's highly possible that a white woman with her white husband's name could have had a mulatto child and still maintained the white man's surname, leaving one of those perplexing genealogical questions. Download the pdf file and spend time using the search feature to see if you can find out anything about your ancestors, black or white.

Unless we find documents, we don't know whether our ancestors had slaves or not. It's not fair to their memory to "assume" that they did. For all we know, they could have been abolitionists. And if we do find a census that shows that an ancestor had a slave, we can't be sure that our ancestor did not "buy" the slave in order to obtain his/her freedom. It is probably not likely and it may seem as though I'm giving our Southern ancestors a ticket out but there were some very kind white people who genuinely abhorred slavery and sometimes bought slaves to keep them from being sold. In some instances, people of color were not allowed to be free, they had to be owned, so kind white people "bought" them but in reality gave them their freedom.

Chapter Nine

THE BOOK OF NEGROES

Three-quarters of the ancestors of today's African Americans were in the colonies by 1776. In the 1870 census, it is unusual to find anyone born in Africa. African Americans have an extremely difficult time tracing their ancestry before the 1800s but *The Book of Negroes*, is one source that may help. It goes back to 1783.

In early July of 1782, the British evacuated Savannah, Georgia. At the end of November, they signed preliminary *Articles of Peace* and in the middle of December they left Charleston, South Carolina. In April of 1783, Congress ratified the peace treaty and by September 3rd, the United States and Great Britain signed the *Treaty of Paris*. On November 25th, British troops left New York City.

"The Book of Negroes was a list compiled by commissioners appointed by the British Commander in Chief, Sir Guy Carleton, as the Loyalists were evacuating New York between April and November 1783. It contains the names and identifying information of African Americans departing with the Loyalists, such information being the basis for any future compensation claims from Patriot slave owners. A copy was sent to Congress. The transcript is taken from the original document held in the National Archives of the United Kingdom."

Care was taken that none of the "Negroes" were property of any United States citizens. I believe they were Loyalists or were evacuated along with the Loyalists and sailed to Nova Scotia. There are many pages of *Inspection Rolls*, where they summarized black passengers. Thousands of black men, women and children left the newly formed United States, bound for British territory.

The book has the copy feature enabled so you'll be able to go through the summaries and copy entries and save them in your own document. Here is an example of what one might do with the records. The following is for the surname *Holmes*:

1783, New York: Sam, 26, stout B fellow. Joseph Holmes of Port Roseway, claimant. (Joseph Holmes).

Property of Joseph Holmes. Jack, 23, stout B fellow. Joseph of Port Roseway, claimant. (Joseph Holmes). Property of Joseph Holmes.

Charles Cambridge, 27, very stout, blacksmith, M, (Joel Holmes). Says he was born free in Worcester County, Maryland; served his time with Joseph Ducheel.

William Homes, 26, stout fellow. Formerly the property of Robert Morris of Philadelphia; left him 5 years ago.

Betsy Holmes, 18, stout wench with 2 children 3 & 1 years of age. Says she was born free.

Emey Addams, 26, likely wench, (Capt. McCoy). Formerly the property of Isaac Homes, John's Island, South Carolina; left him 4 years ago. GBC.

Samuel Holms, 32, ordinary fellow, (Ellias & Eve). Formerly slave to Joseph Holms, Charlestown, South Carolina; left him in 1780

Thomas Holme, 22 years, stout fellow, (Black Brigade). Formerly slave to _____ Cairiores of Charlestown, South Carolina; left him about 7 1/2 years ago.

There's a lot of information here. We have slaves, slave owners and free blacks. We also have spelling variants; Holmes, Homes, Holms and Holme. They come from Maryland, Philadelphia and South Carolina. Let's pick a few names from the list and see what might be waiting for us on the Internet:

The first entry only has Sam and that he is 26 and B, which means black. So I will see what comes up under his "claimant." I will google the following:

Slaves of Joseph Holmes of Port Roseway

I did not find Sam but I could learn a lot about the history of black Loyalists, Port Roseway and slaves with the surname Holmes. If I stuck to it, I just might find something that leads me to Sam.

Let's try the fifth entry, Betsy Holmes. I'm going to put the date and add her name:

1783 Betsy Holmes born free

Once again, a lot of activity. You have to change it up a little or you'll wind up getting the original source. Doing a search for Betsy has brought up a pdf for "Other Free People in Early Barnwell District," by Isabel Vandervelde. It caught my eye because I recognize Barnwell District, South Carolina. Those words are all over my southern family tree. It is a folksy book made with a lot of heart and an impressive knowledge of the descendants. It's a goldmine for anyone with the Holmes surname. It even includes personal correspondence. Here is the first paragraph of the introduction:

"Free Colored Descendants of George Galphin"
"George Galphin, widely known as an Indian Trader who helped the Americans against the British during the American Revolution, is just as widely known among local history buffs for the many children he sired. In his voluminous will he names his children, one by an Indian slave, three by different mulatto slaves, three with Metawney, the daughter of a Creek chief, and two white children with a French girl."

Let's try one more:
1783 Thomas Holme Black Brigade

Not much luck with this name because there was a famous surveyor named Thomas Holmes and his listings are crowding our search. There is nothing worse than a famous person with the same name. It took me about thirty years to filter out an ancestor who shared the same name as a prolific newspaper columnist. But I kept at it. One day, I stumbled across a small obituary that made sense. It not only opened up the world of that ancestor but a gigantic family tree that spanned many surnames for hundreds of years.

Maybe I should have first queried:

What was the Black Brigade of the Revolutionary War?

Wikipedia has this: "The Black Brigade, a combat unit of elite commandos consisting of Black Loyalists, or formerly enslaved African Americans or Free Negroes who escaped to the British during the American Revolutionary War."

Further searching brings up blackpast.org and this:

"Colonel Tye was an escaped slave who fought with the British in the American Revolution. Challenging Patriot forces primarily in New York and New Jersey, Tye became one of the most respected leaders of the Loyalist troops during the Revolution, a respected and feared guerrilla commander... During the winter of 1779, Tye was promoted to commander of a group of twenty-four black Loyalists known as the Black Brigade."

The colonel's original name was Titus, so not the Thomas Holme we're searching for. But there were only twenty-four men in the Black Brigade. Perhaps there is a list out there. With not only Thomas's name on it but someone else's long-lost ancestor as well.

I don't know what avenues you take to uncover your family history. This is the kind of researching I do. One thing leads to another. Sometimes it takes thirty years but sometimes it just appears. As if the ancestor was looking over our shoulder and guiding us.

Chapter Ten

Names, Names, Names…

I have a very southern name… Suellen. There was even a character in the classic movie, *Gone with the Wind*, named Suellen. All my life, I've heard people speak my name with a fake accent because the name made them think… Southern. My mother told me one day that my father wanted to name me April. "Why didn't you?" I asked, to which she answered, "Because I couldn't imagine myself on the porch shouting… *April!*"

I've discovered that during the colonial era, African Americans brought a tradition with them; to name their children after the months they were born. Days, weeks and seasons were also used. Sometimes the month was in the original African language. Eventually, the names were Anglicized. If you run across an ancestor's name and it looks like it might be African, you might be able to find out what region of Africa they came from by researching the months, days and seasons of the various African languages. That sounds like a lot of work but it would be a great story to tell and valuable heritage uncovered.

In the census of 2000, the top twelve most prevalent surnames for African Americans are as follows: **Williams, Johnson, Smith, Jones, Brown, Jackson, Davis, Thomas, Harris, Robinson, Taylor and Wilson.** There are almost 2,000 surnames listed. If most of your ancestors are white, it's frustrating to look at your genealogical paperwork and try to guess which one *might* be black. It would be a rare instance to tell by looking at a name but if you are trying to identify which ancestors in your tree are black, this list is beneficial, even if all it gives you is hope to keep looking. It has a search feature at the top but it is a "public records search" and will lead you astray. Instead, use the search feature on your own computer and "find on this page." Type in the surname of the ancestor that you are researching. The list will show you how many black people identify with that name. Perhaps the higher on the list the name is, the higher your odds of that person being black. It's a way of narrowing things down.

Let's say you have an ancestor whose name is William Thompson Hargrove. You have him singled out as *maybe* being a person of color on your family tree that you'd like to identify. You've never figured out why he has the middle name of Thompson. Isn't that more of a last name? Out of curiosity, you search for Thompson and find that it is number 19 on the list and that 145,176 people with that surname self-identify as "black." Over twenty-two percent of people with the last name Thompson on the 2000 census self-identify as "black."

Let's look at one of the uncommon surnames, Ivery. It's almost at the bottom of the list of nearly 2,000 surnames but over eighty-nine percent of Iverys on the census self-identify as "black." That's an amazingly high percentage and an excellent clue. One that would make any genealogist ecstatic. It's a fun list to play with. Here is the link: http://names.mongabay.com/data/black.html.

There are countless websites designed to help genealogists search for black ancestry. The problem that I have with them is that they are so detailed and offer so many possibilities that for someone with nothing but a name, all that information is overwhelming. They provide invaluable information and those who donate their time to build the websites are heroic but I tend to gravitate toward lists where I can type in a surname and then if I find something, build on what I have found.

I can't stress this enough. *Let your intuition be your guide.* Have faith and just keep following one hunch after the other. If the ancestors are looking over your shoulder… you'll find it.

Chapter Eleven

And if You Can't Find 'em...
There's Always the Natchez Trace

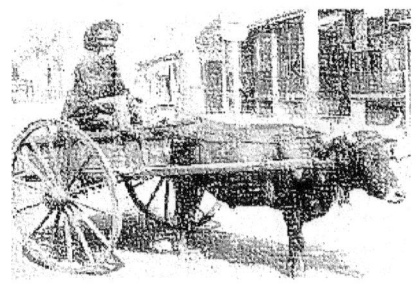

One of my favorite aspects of writing genealogy books is the freedom to speculate. Our ancestors are dead now and sometimes we're lucky just to know their names. Knowing the locations where they lived is a blessing. We can go there on vacation and fantasize about what their lives must have been like, which is what a lot of us do because we have little else to go on. Genealogy is full of stories, often built on not much more than a location and our imagination. Sometimes it is all we have.

What triggers the emotions that make genealogists want to unravel the stories of their ancestors? It might be because it's natural for our brains to want to fill in the missing pieces. And participating in surname chat rooms and gathering information on great-great-grandma is gossiping, isn't it? It's a well-known fact among psychologists that gossiping boosts levels of the hormone serotonin, thereby lowering anxiety and stress levels. Serotonin is one of those feel-good chemicals that's released through bonding. There's plenty of bonding between genealogists researching the same surnames. They call each other "cousin." I see no reason why we can't bond with our dead ancestors. The more I discover about them, the more I feel connected to them. When I started discovering my ancestors, it brought lots of positive feelings. It definitely boosted my self-esteem. I'm willing to admit that a lot of it was probably my imagination but to this day, I look at myself differently and I never look in the mirror without thinking of the chain of people who came before me. If I feel connected to my adult children who live far away, who's to say I'm not connected to my ancestors?

The serotonin producing effect explains some of the addiction of genealogy. That and storytelling. I write fiction and a lot of what I write is taken from real life. What really inspires me to write stories is when I visit the locations where my ancestors subsisted. One of those inspirational places is the Natchez Trace Parkway, *a 444-mile drive through exceptional scenery and 10,000 years of North*

American history. Used by American Indians, 'Kaintucks,'
settlers, and future presidents, the Old Trace played an
important role in American history, states the National Parks
brochure.

Although close to the border, the Natchez Trace is not in
Louisiana but it is not terribly far from New Orleans. It
began as a Native American footpath where the Indians
followed migrating bison. By the 1700's, it was the fastest
way to get between the Cumberland Gap plateau (Virginia,
Kentucky and Tennessee), the Mississippi River, the Gulf of
Mexico (Pensacola Florida), Mobile Alabama and New
Orleans. Farmers from the north loaded their flat-boats with
produce and floated down the river to sell their produce at
the markets in New Orleans. They took the flat-boats apart
and sold the logs and took the Natchez Trace home,
sometimes all the way to Pittsburgh, Pennsylvania.

The Natchez Trace has every element. Big plantations, trade
opportunities, shipping access over both water and land.
Huge agricultural areas where farmers from Kentucky and
Ohio could easily come down the Mississippi with their
commodities and then (not as easily) walk or take a wagon
back. Criss-crossing several states, it was a trader's dream.

Used by the French, the Spanish, Caribbean slaves, African slaves, the Irish, the English, Canadians and Native Americans. Talk about a melting pot. And amongst the multitudes of travelers and traders, what better way for someone to assimilate?

One of our mulatto ancestors could have used metropolitan Natchez to blend in with other dark-skinned immigrants. Plenty of Native Americans claimed they were Black Dutch, Black German or Black Irish. Maybe those with African ancestors made similar claims. If their patriarchal line ran Dutch, German or Irish and their matriarchal line ran from Africa, why not call yourself Black Dutch? Today there are people on genealogy sites asking the question… what is Black Irish? What is Black Dutch? What's a Black German? There are probably many answers. But to be sure, that answer includes people who were reassigning their ethnicity to one that provided more freedom.

Anyone could have wound up in Natchez. There was a slave market, so slaves from all over the world could have passed through there. The Natchez Trace went up to the Ohio River. It went through Mississippi, Tennessee and connected with Kentucky and West Virginia. Dutch Farmers from Kentucky came down the Trace. Before they were in Kentucky, those Dutch Farmers lived back east. And before that, Holland. Before that, Spain and Portugal. Before that maybe the Holy Land.

In 2011, my husband and I rode a motorcycle up the Natchez Trace. We stopped and saw markers for historical Indian Mounds. We rode into Nashville and eventually found our way up to Cleveland, Ohio and Lake Erie. Up at the Great Lakes, the ancient interlocking networks of footpaths that became the popular route to the Natchez Trace unites us with the French Canadians and their strong connections with the Natives. Germans and Scandinavians who settled in the Great Lakes region also had farmers who flat-boated down the Mississippi River and went home via the trace. America was truly a melting pot. We are the left over stew. Our ancestors were everybody and everywhere.

The next time you look at your family tree and see blank spots or the name of an ancestor you know nothing about, think of the Natchez Trace. There's a good chance they or their ancestors passed through it. Instead of saying, "I can't find them," how about saying, "I'm still looking at the

Natchez Trace." Genealogy… why do we love it? It's full of story-telling. Natchez *definitely* has its share.

— —

Chapter Twelve

What Should We Look Like? What Do We Look Like?

Hamite – *noun*

1. A descendant of Ham, Noah's second son. Found in the Bible, *Genesis* 6 – 20.

2. A member of the chief native race of North Africa. The Hamites are Caucasians, characterized by tall stature, dark, or even black skin, wavy hair, and oval face.

Years ago, I visited an Indian Reservation and was surprised at the different colors of hair and skin. And they were all Indians. They were the result of centuries of admixture. We don't expect all Native Americans, all white people or all black people to look the same. Or any other ethnic group. But there was a time when our ancestors had only admixed with neighboring tribes and they had a distinctive look. We might be shocked to see our ancestors from the 1400s. No doubt, sometimes we would resemble them and other times we would be convinced they had nothing to do with our being. But they did.

In the early 1800's, the Underground Railroad was established, allowing fugitive slaves with enough luck and assistance to make their way to destinations in Ontario, Canada, where as mentioned earlier, they sometimes intermarried with the Irish. Today, the Irish figure largely in many a multi-ethnic family tree. Thinking back to the Indian Reservation, I saw a lot of evidence of Irish ethnicity in the Indian children with fair skin, freckles and red hair. A street sign bears the name Henderson. A Scottish and Northern Irish surname.

What physical characteristics or attributes do you have that make you curious? There is one stereotype that I wonder about... dancing. African Americans are seen in great number out on the dance floor. Yes, yes... white people are all over the dance floors too but I do wonder when I'm at a wedding dancing and my sister and her daughters are all out on the floor with me dancing. And my cousin from New

Orleans told me that our southern grandmother used to do a "little jig." Thinking about these things makes genealogy fun. I'm not saying that white people can't dance and black people can. But I am asking… are black people more inclined to want to dance? And enjoy doing it? If you do an Internet search, "The cultural differences between whites and blacks regarding dancing," you'll find a lot of discussion. Maybe people with southern roots enjoying dancing, white or black. But when you are *really* curious and suspicious that someone is keeping something from you… it's the little things that spur your attention, even if you laugh after the thought.

Speaking of little things that make us suspicious, my grandmother had a parasol. If you are the least bit suspicious and you see a picture of her with a parasol, one wonders if she was trying to stay out of the sun because it darkened her skin, revealing black ancestry. White Southern women with traces of black ancestry may have spent their afternoons on the porch, away from the sun. When I questioned my uncle about our ancestry, one of the things he said was, "We were all very white." What an odd thing to say. Why would someone volunteer that? I could see for myself that all the family had white skin. But there was something characteristic in the way my grandmother and aunts spoke. If I was hearing their voices on the radio and didn't see them, I might think they were black. One day I told my mother, "I always thought Mamaw (popular southern word for grandmother) and her daughters sounded like black women." She was surprised at the question regarding her in-laws, "I always thought so too but I never said anything."

There is a theory that the southern accent grew out of a mixture of English-speaking free children playing with the children of slaves on the plantation. If that is true, then anyone with a southern accent sounds "black." What does a black person sound like? Is it different from that of a white person? Frequently, but not always. Is it physical or is it cultural? A discussion on the website Quora gave some interesting responses. One was that black people tended to be larger. Larger jaws and vocal chords might play a part. Another was that speaking is a remnant of the language spoken by our ancestors. One black man's response was that black voices have an "organic rumble tone." He claims high accuracy at picking out white and black voices.

What is someone with African origins supposed to look like? I looked it up because honestly, I did not know because black

Americans are extremely diverse. I guess I wanted a cheat sheet. We know that Africans have dark-colored skin, from brown to black. But how dark it is, depends on the amount of skin pigmentation someone has. Melanin levels are much higher closer to the equator. It's nature's way of protecting skin from the sun. African's eyes are very dark and their hair is black, often coarse and tightly curled. A long cranium (skull/head) is common (dolichocephalic). Noses are flat and broad, as are other ethnic groups from hot climates, including the Mediterranean. Men might not have as much facial or body hair. The lips are thick, especially the bottom lip and much more prominent than most whites.

Living near the equator requires a different set of physical adaptations. The African sun is unforgiving. Nature helps humans survive the strong ultraviolet rays by building skin pigmentation. It works as a natural sunscreen by deflecting the sunlight away. So does tight curly hair.

The exact opposite is happening with people who live far north above the equator, in Scandinavia. Their skin is fair because it has been *de-pigmented*. The reason for this is black skin with its heavy pigment would deflect the sun's ultraviolet rays and that would be a very bad thing for people living in the cold, dark north. Vitamin D is made when bare skin is exposed to sunlight, helped along by the oils in our skin. (Harsh bathing can strip our skin of its natural oils resulting in not enough production of those vitamins.)

Let's take a look at the difference in nose structure. Although the Berbers are known for their "thin noses," many people of African descent have flat broad noses whereas many from a cold northern climate have a thin nose to prevent the intake of large blasts of freezing cold air. Thinking I was doing a healthy thing, more than once I made the mistake of inhaling freezing cold air into my lungs. I thought it was good old-fashioned fresh air but my lungs did not like it.

Quote

"… scientists do not associate ancestries with skin color at all, and instead see groups of skeletal morphologies as indicative of the population inhabiting a certain area of the world. For example, a certain combination of traits such as a broad nasal aperture and wide interorbital breadth is more common in peoples that originate from the continent of Africa, and can be seen in populations that stem from this area, including African Americans and black South Africans… The opposing traits of a narrow nasal aperture and interorbital breadth are more indicative of a population whose ancestors adapted to the environments of Europe, such as European Americans and white South Africans, both groups descending from European colonists..."

"Estimating Ancestry in South Africa: A Comparison of Geometric Morphometrics and Traditional Craniometrics," page 4, by Rebecca Elizabeth King

If you're a European American looking in the mirror and you are looking for features that might give hints of African ancestry, look for a flat wide nose, prominent eyes, prominent forward leaning lips and a more prominent center in the forehead. Forensic anthropologists say that the face (meaning the skull) is the best at determining ancestry.

No matter the color of our skin or the shape of our nose, we have all been sculpted by nature and helped along to adapt to new climates as we migrated for tens of thousands of years. A lot of black people in the Western world have a wide nose and bigger lips, but there are also black people who have thin lips. There are white people who have thick lips. I guess we look like what we are supposed to look like... us... and those who came before us.

Interesting Websites

DEFUSING THE HAMITE-NEGRO-NILOTE CONCEPTION

http://www.africaspeaks.com/reasoning/index.php?topic=1059.0;wap2

Dahomey, a precolonial West African kingdom - SLAVE KINGDOMS EPISODE

www.pbs.org/wonders/Episodes/Epi3/3_wondr2.htm

The Louisiana Division of New Orleans Public Library has an alphabetical card file of more than 650,000 names, called *The Louisiana Biography and Obituary Index*. It references obituaries and death notices published in New Orleans newspapers from 1804-1972 and biographical information published in older Louisiana collective biographies.

http://nutrias.org/~nopl/obits/obits.htm

LARGE SLAVEHOLDERS OF 1860 and AFRICAN AMERICAN SURNAME MATCHES FROM 1870 by Tom Blake, 2001-2005

http://freepages.genealogy.rootsweb.ancestry.com/~ajac/

SLAVERY IN THE NORTH

http://www.slavenorth.com/index.html

Africa and the American Negro: Addresses and Proceedings
of the Congress on Africa, 1895:
http://docsouth.unc.edu/church/bowen/bowen.html

Black History in Canada
http://www.blackhistorycanada.ca/events.php?themeid=21
&id=6

http://www.pbs.org/wgbh/aia/part1/1narr3.html

For extensive information, including maps: Slave Trade and
African   American   Ancestry
http://wysinger.homestead.com/mapofafricadiaspora.html

Bibliography

The American Red Cross

http://m.redcrossblood.org/learn-about-blood/blood-types

ANCIENT AND RECENT DEMOGRAPHIC EVENTS INFLUENCE MITOCHONDRIAL DNA DIVERSITY IN AN IMMIGRANT BASQUE POPULATION, by Michael Christopher Davis, Boise State University, December 2010.

"Berbers," Grolier Encyclopedia, Volumes 3 & 4, The Grolier Society, Inc. 1956.

BIOLOGICAL DISTANCE AND THE AFRICAN AMERICAN DENTITION, By Heather Joy Hecht Edgar, M.A., The Ohio State University, 2002.

THE BOOK OF NEGROES

http://www.blackloyalist.info/sourcedetail/display/15

http://www.ox.ac.uk/news/2015-03-24-complex-genetic-ancestry-americans-uncovered-0

http://crab.rutgers.edu/~glasker/DIFFERENTAFRICANS2003.htm

The Dutch in Indonesia
https://en.wikipedia.org/wiki/Dutch_East_India_Company_in_Indonesia

ESTIMATING ANCESTRY IN SOUTH AFRICA: A COMPARISON OF GEOMETRIC MORPHOMETRICS AND TRADITIONAL CRANIOMETRICS, by REBECCA ELIZABETH KING, BOSTON UNIVERSITY SCHOOL OF MEDICINE, 2015.

FINDING A PLACE CALLED HOME (A Guide To African~American Genealogy and Historical Identity), Dee Farmer WOODTOR, Ph. D., 1999.

http://www.forumbiodiversity.com/showthread.php/1996-What-nations-are-most-rachycephalic-and-most-dolichocephalic

Information on African Americans on the Federal Census:
https://www.archives.gov/research/census/african-american/census-1790-1930.pdf

https://www.sott.net/article/263587-DNA-shows-Irish-people-have-more-complex-origins-than-previously-thought

https://www.theguardian.com/science/2015/dec/28/origins-of-the-irish-down-to-mass-migration-ancient-dna-confirms

The Journal of the Royal Asiatic Society of Great Britain and Ireland, Volume 3 ,page 109 – 110:
https://books.google.com/books?id=vsMsAAAAIAAJ&pg=PA109&lpg=PA109&dq=Mazirgh&source=bl&ots=23H9zYqQVT&sig=5ARaTyb5UqTYCEHexF_I9x7k1Pk&hl=en&sa=X&ved=0ahUKEwi6j-_niLDNAhUI7WMKHWaPDXY4ChDoAQgeMAE#v=onepage&q=Mazirgh&f=false

"LANDMARKS OF DETROIT, A HISTORY OF THE CITY," by Robert B. Ross and George B. Catlin, The Evening News Association, Detroit 1898.
https://archive.org/stream/landmarksofdetro00ross/landmarksofdetro00ross_djvu.txt

Mississippi Slave Narratives from the WPA Records

http://theusgenweb.org/ms/slaves/harris-xslave.htm

http://names.mongabay.com/data/black.html

OTHER FREE PEOPLE IN EARLY BARNWELL DISTRICT, by Isabel Vandervelde, Art Studio Press, 240 Newberry N.W., Aiken, S.C., 2001.

SECULAR CHANGE IN THE SKULL BETWEEN AMERICAN BLACKS AND WHITES, by Nicole Danielle Truesdell, The Department of Geography and Anthropology, Louisiana State University, May, 2005.

SLAVERY PETITIONS:
http://academic.lexisnexis.com/documents/upa_cis/16456_ RSFBSlaveryPetitionsSerIIPt%20D.pdf, BLACK STUDIES RESEARCH SOURCES, General Editor: John H. Bracey, Jr., RACE, SLAVERY AND FREE BLACKS, Edited by Loren Schweninger, 2005.

THREE-DIMENSIONAL PHOTOGRAPHY OF FACIAL MORPHOLOGY OF AFRICAN-AMERICAN CHILDREN COMPARED TO WELSH CHILDREN by

DON FRANKLIN NORRIS, The University of Alabama at Birmingham, 2014.

A WORK OF COMPASSION? Dutch slavery and slave trade in the Indian Ocean in the seventeenth century, by Markus P. M. Vink.
http://www.historycooperative.org/proceedings/seascapes/vink.html

https://en.m.wikipedia.org/wiki/Georgian_Jews

https://en.m.wikipedia.org/wiki/Georgia_(country)

https://en.m.wikipedia.org/wiki/Principality_of_Iberia#

https://en.wikipedia.org/wiki/Dahomey

https://en.wikipedia.org/wiki/Charity_Hospital_(New_Orleans)

https://en.m.wikipedia.org/wiki/History_of_the_Jews_in_Iran

www.ingramcontent.com/pod-product-compliance
Lightning Source LLC
Chambersburg PA
CBHW071209280526
45787CB00002B/616